Contents

Podcasting Made Easy videos: https://bit.ly/2GcxEhU

Introduction

Hello and welcome to the 2nd edition of *Podcasting Made Easy*. Podcasting is an increasingly popular way for people to share news and information about their business, hobbies and interests.

Audio files are a lot smaller than video files, so are easier and quicker to share. Podcasts can also be enjoyed while on the move – they don't require people to look at a screen. For this reason they are versatile and can be enjoyed during almost any activity.

My first podcast was made in 2009 when I started a weekly review of business and stock market news linked to a magazine I was editing.

Later I moved on to podcasting about careers and employment, and then a weekly news podcast called *Talking Point*. In 2014 I started a one-hour news podcast that was syndicated to dozens of internet and low power FM radio stations across the US, New Zealand and the UK (in addition to being on all the best podcatching sites).

So quite a few podcasts over the years, each one running its course, and some overlapping one another.

My background is in journalism, and during the 80s/90s I worked in radio, so I have been able to use some of the best gear there is. But from my home office / studio, I started podcasting using modest equipment.

I routinely browse the podcast forums and read heated debates on which microphone is 'best', which mixer is better than another, learn about people's favourite software, and so on.

My view is that content comes first, audio quality a close second and then the gear. I am a bit fanatical about audio being clean so listeners aren't turned off by poor audio quality. But it was only recently that I got anything near pro gear – most of my podcasts have been recorded using a budget mic and free software. Once I knew podcasting was for me I started to invest in better gear to up my game.

I think of it like this; does having a top-notch camera make one a better photographer? No. Most of the art of a good photo comes down to experience, technique, composition, and skill. The same applies to any trade. So when it comes to podcasting, while a certain level of audio quality is expected by listeners – because they are used to digital recordings and FM / DAB radio – you don't need to spend a king's ransom just to make a podcast.

One podcaster I know still uses an old goose neck microphone that came free with his PC 10 years ago. It sounds like it too. But still, the content is good and he has built up a keen following.

And that is the basic premise of *Podcasting Made Easy*, to help you make great podcasts with as little initial outlay as possible, and help you understand why you would want to podcast at all.

I believe the basics required to be a successful podcaster are a passion to communicate and commitment to the subject matter of your podcast – the rest will fall into place as your audience builds and your skill level improves. Passion and desire must come first.

Use what you have at hand and do it anyway.

What is a podcast?

A podcast is an audio recording that is made available for free via podcast libraries such as Apple, TuneIn, and Spreaker etc.

POD stands for Play On Demand, and there is a podcast for most any subject you can think of.

Some radio broadcasters release shows, or segments of shows, as downloadable files, and there is some debate among the podcast community as to whether the podcast tag really applies to them – I don't think it does.

In my opinion, podcasts are defined as a sequence of speech-based recordings where someone shares their expertise/information on a given subject at regular intervals – typically weekly.

Some people talk about comic book characters, TV shows, films... You name it – if it exists (in the real world or not) there's bound to be a podcast about it. But don't let that stop you starting your own one.

So, if you want to start getting 'on the air' to share your thoughts and expertise, the following pages cover everything you need to get started and take your podcast to its full potential.

Good luck.

Why podcast?

First off, you need to decide why you want to start podcasting. Do you just fancy the idea of being heard around the world? Is it an ego trip, do you want to do it just because you can, do you want to raise your profile or drum up business?

If you are employed, and being paid by your boss to host a podcast for the firm, then you're laughing. You'll get paid to do something that can be great fun – and you shouldn't have to worry about the cost of setting it all up.

But if you are in business and only really get paid when a client pays you then you will need to dig deep to find the stamina to podcast week in, week out. There has to be a benefit to the cost in time and effort for doing it. Fame is great if that's what you want, but fortune is better.

From what I have seen, most of the people who just fancy the idea of podcasting, and who don't really have a game plan, abandon the idea before they have completed 10 episodes.

In fact, many podcasts don't make it to seven episodes for this very reason. This is because after the initial buzz of making the first few shows has subsided, making a podcast can become a chore, a chore with little reward – just the self-appointed kudos of having recorded a show and uploaded it for distribution.

Then you find that only 30 people downloaded your last podcast, you get zero feedback from listeners (who are more fickle and disengaged than you would ever imagine), your calls for donations via a PayPal 'donate' button to keep the show 'on the air' falls on deaf ears, and slowly you begin to wonder why you are doing it at all. Which is the key question. Why?

Yes, making a podcast is great fun, but why are you doing it? Just because you can? Not good enough!

If you fancy a career in broadcasting, then maybe fronting a podcast is one way to get some exposure and experience of speaking into a microphone, interviewing people, producing a show, adding music, and dropping in jingles.

It could help form a showreel for you to send to radio stations, and in this case, falls under the 'market your brand / raise your profile' subject heading.

But it does take a lot of time, and it's not quite the same as being live on air – it could make for a good experience nonetheless. In which case; host your shows for free on Mixcloud.com which covers royalty payments for you.

To be honest though, there are plenty of hospital and internet radio stations around crying out for people to volunteer their time to host shows, and if you fancy that then see:
www.forum.internet–radio.com/volunteering/

Trawl through the podcasts on Apple's Podcast app, TuneIn, Spreaker, Stitcher etc and you'll quickly figure out that the vast majority of podcasts are made by people with something to sell, and use their podcast to promote their products or services by sharing their insights and expertise. They promote themselves as being experts in their field as a marketing operation.

So, what's your area of expertise or passion? What can you talk about to friends without a moment's thought? In short, what subject do you know inside out, enjoy keeping abreast of and talking about?

Okay, so you may have a hobby you can talk about, and it may also be that you hope to turn that hobby into a paying job at some point. You could talk for 10 minutes each week on the latest news from within your industry.

The bottom line is, what's in it for you? Are you podcasting for your employer on their dime [great]? Or are you podcasting for personal reasons? Either way, you must decide where you are going before you start.

Lock down these four words before you start:
- Vision: Blue sky thinking on where you want to be
- Goal: The desired result, a specific place
- Plan: The steps you need to take to achieve your goal
- Purpose: Why? The reason for all of the above (more sales?)

Key take away
Want to start a podcast? Why now and why you?

Who listens to podcasts?

Podcasts have been around since 2004. Adam Curry and Dave Winer are credited with doing the first one, and writer Ben Hammersley (of UK newspaper *The Guardian*) is credited with first using the term podcasting. There is even an International Podcasting Day (30 September).

There are millions of hours of podcasts produced every year, the audience for them is building fast, and that has been well established by Edison Research in numerous annual surveys it has carried out with Triton Digital.

Edison Research's Podcast Consumer 2019 survey (North America) reveals the audience for podcasting grew significantly in 2018. It says half (51%) of all Americans aged 12+ have listened to a podcast.

In addition, podcasting's Share of Ear has more than doubled in five years, increasing 122% since 2014.

Although all key demographics grew, much of the increase in podcasting (in the US) has come from people aged 12 to 24.

Forty-one percent of monthly podcast listeners say they are listening to more podcasts today than a year ago.

Streaming services are playing a role in the growth of podcasting, with 43% of monthly podcast listeners saying they have listened to a podcast on Spotify, and 35% on Pandora.

Music is the number one topic in terms of interest from podcast consumers according to the survey.

Of all US podcast consumers who took part in the survey, 54% say they are more likely to consider the brands they hear advertised on podcasts, compared to 7% who say they are less likely.

Other results of its 2019 Infinite Dial survey in the US show that:

- 144 million people in the US have listened to a podcast
- 90 million people in the US listen to a podcast every week
- The male / female split is 36 million male / 29 million female
- Ages are: 12-17 (10%); 18-34 (39%); 35-54 (35%); 55+ (16%)
- Race composition: white (66%); African American (11%); Hispanic (9%); Asian (4%); Other (7%); Refused to state (3%)
- Annual income of listeners: USD$75,000 to $150,000

- Number of podcasts listened to last week: One (16% of people); two (15%); three (17%); four (21%)
- Where did people listen to a podcast? At home (90%); in a car/truck (64%); walking around (49%); at the gym (43%); at work (37%); while on public transport (37%)

All the available evidence points to a rosy future for podcasting – which means any doubt you had about podcasting being a worthwhile venture should be extinguished.

It is also clear that people earning well above average annual incomes will be your audience. The downside is they don't like to spend time downloading and listening to a podcast only for it to be full of sales pitches. They prefer ad-free or ad-light podcasts.

People who like listening to podcasts also listen to them more than they do other forms of audio, such as radio and music. They are a captive audience that's fully engaged with the medium.

One note I did see toward the end of Edison's 2017 survey report was that content isn't king, the audience is king. The report writer, in an almost throw-away line, says: "There are huge under-served potential audiences for new forms of spoken word media – so let's not rely on 'received wisdom' too much."

As a writer I'd always say content is king because it is the content that is sought out by consumers. But if consumers are king (the customer is always right), podcasters wanting the largest audience need to give them what they want.

I'd counter though that any content will find an audience, the audience you want is one that has an affinity with what you have to say.

Sources:
www.edisonresearch.com/the-podcast-consumer-2019/
www.edisonresearch.com/the-podcast-consumer-2017/
www.edisonresearch.com/podcast-consumer-australia-2017/

Key take away
There's gold in them thar hills! But it's quite a journey.

Ideal duration of a podcast

How long should each episode of a podcast run for? There are no hard and fast rules, and there are plenty that run for an hour or two. Others feature snippets of information in shows that last for 10 minutes or less – an audio snack that delivers key information in the shortest possible time. It's the podcast gone tabloid.

I believe the content should decide the duration. Some weeks you may do a 10 minute podcast, other weeks half an hour.

But, to keep people's attention for half an hour or more the content has to be pretty compelling. Think about it, how long do you actively listen to a radio show before your mind wanders or you get up to do something else? That is your personal yardstick.

And consider this, the average journey time for someone going to work is between 15 and 25 minutes. The beauty of podcasts is that people frequently listen to them while on the move, the smartphone is the new portable radio, and internet access in cars is becoming standardised with radios able to access internet radio and podcast sites.

Because people don't generally have an hour to spare, nor are many of us up to the job of holding someone's attention for that long, I believe the optimum duration of a podcast must be between five and 20 minutes.

And while podcasts can offer pure entertainment, some of it very funny and hosted by well known names, the podcasts I am most interested in feature information that people can use. And if you can share it quickly, then do so – your listeners will thank you for it.

Now if you plan to do a much longer show, then look at the formula of the magazine news shows on TV. They spend about 8 minutes on each topic. There's an intro/explainer, an interview, a round up and conclusion. Then it is on to the next item (it takes a lot of work).

When I listen to a podcast I need to know 'what's in it for me?'. What am I being offered that I can't get anywhere else, and how much time do I have to give away to get it? Too many people are time poor.

Making a short podcast is a lot easier than making a long one – obvious I know – so start as you mean to go on.

Shorter is easier

A few years back I started to produce a one hour news show. It was basically a podcast that was also broadcast by internet stations. I promoted it as such on radio forums and had quite a few takers.

That one hour of news and interviews was pieced together during the working week in my spare time and took around eight solid hours to complete each episode.

Shorter podcasts can be quick to produce, edit and prepare for distribution. Shorter shows translate into smaller MP3 file sizes, which mean you can store more of them in the cloud (if storage space is limited) and you'll upload them faster. Your listeners will download them faster too.

Being a podcaster means you enter the entertainment arena. And the competition for people's ears is fierce. The shorter your podcast the greater chance it has of being listened to from start to finish. The greater chance you have of developing a following of people who subscribe to your show and listen every week.

Time is money, so cut the waffle, delete the chit chat, stick to the facts (but keep it conversational) and give your audience a breath of fresh air.

Keep your podcasts clean, simple and brief while also letting your personality come through – you are not a newsreader and your personality will give your podcasts the X factor.

Key take away
Keep your podcasts short and to the point. Don't be like a newsreader.

Top and tail

I don't know why, but too many podcasts have music / jingle intros that last for a minute or more, it is something that really bugs me.

Sometimes I have been listening to a podcast for three minutes before the show proper actually starts and I will routinely just stop listening for this reason alone.

Let's be clear; if someone has subscribed and downloaded your podcast, they more or less know what they are going to get. It's not like they just turned on the radio and aren't sure what programme they have happened upon.

If someone has downloaded your podcast then you don't need to keep selling it to them – they've already bought it.

Keep your introduction short and to the point.

For example: "This is [your name] and welcome to this week's [name of podcast] – you can find full show notes at [your website] – this is episode 26. In this week's show we have..."

If you want to use a piece of music to help brand your show, grab a short piece of (royalty free) music – 5 to 15 seconds or so. But do start speaking to your listener within five seconds of them hitting the play button.

Your intro really does set the scene for the podcast, but try not to fall into the trap of a highly polished, processed/loud intro that's followed by a podcast that doesn't match the loudness or quality of the intro – your show will sound flat by comparison.

Keep the intro consistent with the rest of the show as they need to work well together. Try not to let the intro overpower your show or set your listeners up for disappointment.

Consider that many people – down the track – will listen to a few of your podcasts in one hit as they get up to speed. And listening to the same long drawn-out intro over and over can, and will, turn them off.

Your intro can include a quick overview of what's coming up in this edition, mention any special guests appearing in the show and encourage people to subscribe using any of the podcast libraries your show is listed on.

At the end of the show you have a bit of freedom to thank listeners for subscribing and downloading the podcast, prompt new listeners to subscribe and ask them to leave a review and add a star rating. Positive reviews, such as a five star endorsement, really helps raise your podcast to a more prominent position on podcast distribution platforms.

If possible, promote your next show.

"Next week we will be covering XYZ and our special guest will be Jon Doe from ABC company. We'll be chatting about ...."

Ideally you will have already recorded the interview for next week's show.

And this is also a good point to ask listeners to share your posts and podcast on social media. The value of sharing on social media cannot be understated and will help build your followers. It is essential you put a lot of effort into social media to market your shows.

Key take away
Keep your intro short and encourage social media shares.

Behind the mic

When it comes to being 'on air' try to be yourself. Don't pretend to be like someone you hear on the radio with their apparent deep rich voice that's heavily compressed and digitally processed (sometimes beyond anything that sounds natural).

Try not to copy someone else's style (they've already done that) – be true to your voice and personality. Even if you do try to adopt an on-air persona, the mask will fall soon enough.

Sure, you can use elements of what other people do, but add it to your personal mix to avoid mimicking them and risk listeners thinking "Oh, he's trying to sound like that other guy". Don't be that guy.

If you are honest with your listeners it will come through in the recording, and you won't trip up as much while speaking. Because if you are too busy trying to sound and act like someone else, or how you think you should sound, then the content will suffer – because your mind won't be where it needs to be – on the subject at hand or the words you are saying.

Talk about what you know, say it in your own voice, be honest with yourself and your audience.

Embrace diversity. If you have a particular accent, or pronounce certain words in a particular way then so be it. So long as what you say is understandable then you are on your way.

The worst thing you can do is speak too fast, mumble and ramble. That is easily fixed with practice. Slow down, enunciate. Put thought into what you are saying. Pronounce the beginning and the end of the words. Diction is important, but not a deal breaker. You can fix a lot of issues in post production (takes time though).

It is easy for the passion to overtake you, but if you are talking about business and finance or your company's products then a more conservative tone might be better. A tone that lets the listener know you are dealing in matters of facts and information (as opposed to personal opinion).

The tone of your delivery can convey a lot, and if you deliver materially important information in a slap dash Devil-may-care manner then your audience may lose confidence and trust in you and the information you are sharing.

And this leads to another delivery decision for you. Do you report news and information – without comment and in a dry formal manner – or allow your personality come through with a bit of commentary and banter?

Of course, don't fall into the trap of taking yourself too seriously. But do think about your target audience and pitch your delivery with them in mind as well as the content you are sharing.

When it comes to making contact with your listener it pays to talk to your microphone as if it were a person – your best friend perhaps (some people stick a photo of their partner on the mic to help them). That way you can share your news in a natural, conversational style.

Yes, many people may hear your podcast, but each one will likely listen in isolation. And even if a room full of people are listening, each person will listen in their own way.

Remember also that your podcasts – once released to the world – will be around forever more (no pressure). They will sit in people's collections all around the world, each person may listen to it numerous times and share it via all manner of social channels.

And what may be trite and funny to you today, may be an embarrassment tomorrow, or next year, or in five years' time when you have a different job.

If in doubt, leave it out. Keep it clean, don't be offensive, keep it friendly and think how your podcast reflects on you, your personal brand, your employer and the company.

Key take away
Be yourself on air and let your personality shine through.

begins, and this job never ends. But a crowd draws a crowd, and as your podcast gains in popularity so more people will come. Try not to look at your download stats for a few weeks. You will likely be disappointed.

Top tips
- Listen for plosives – the popping sound your microphone can make when you say P words too close to it. A pop filter can reduce/cure this, or turn your head away from the mic as you start a P word
- Keep your recording levels well out of the red zone
- Even out the levels in post production, this can be done manually or you may be able to apply an audio filter (compression) to do this. But don't over do the compression (less is more)
- Ensure each episode of the podcast is the same audio level; Normalise to -1db. Your regular listeners will appreciate the consistency
- A file format of 64kbps, mono at 44.1khz is fine for speech-only podcasts (I use 96kbps for slightly higher quality). If featuring lots of music then export the MP3 at 128kbps, stereo, 44.1khz
- Each MP3 should have correct and consistent meta tag data applied
- The logo for your MP3 should be optimised to reduce the file size

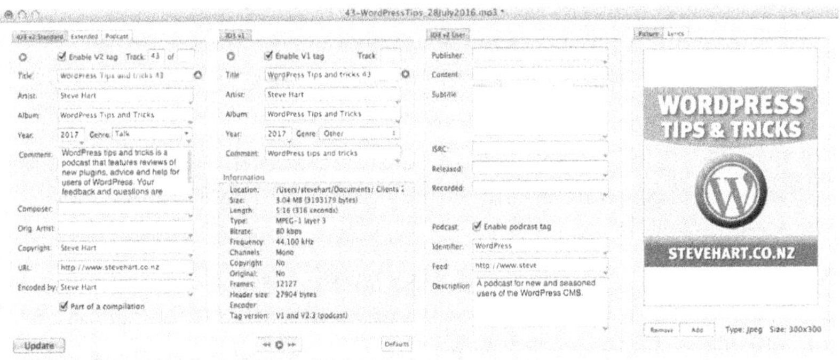

An ID3 editor allows you to add title, artist, and a logo to your MP3 file.

Podcast production

You have probably already worked out that a podcast that lasts for 10 minutes will not take 10 minutes to produce, upload and share online.

My rough guide is that talk-based podcasting can take around 10 minutes for each finished minute. Because there is the preparation to get your thoughts and notes together before you sit in front of the microphone. Then you need to record it. Record it again because of the mistakes you made the first time, post production [editing out mouth clicks, erms and ahs], polish and add intro/outro music.

Then you need to export and convert your finished recording to MP3, listen to the podcast, add meta data to the MP3 file, upload it to the hosting firm's server, create a web page (post) for the episode on your website, write show notes and then publish to release your podcast to all the podcast libraries you have submitted your podcast feed to.

Depending on how polished you want your recording to be, your 10-minute podcast could take two hours of your life every week.

Equipment

Boy, we could write a whole book on the equipment options for podcasters. But let's get one thing straight – all you really need is a quiet room, a microphone, computer (or a good quality digital recorder), recording/editing software, and the ability to save your recording as an MP3 (mono 64k is common for a speech-based podcast).

Ideally you will also have ID3 tag software. This allows you to add cover art/logo to your MP3 file (a nice touch), as well as add 'hidden' meta data such as show name, episode number, your podcast feed URL, and copyright information etc.

As for audio hardware…sure, there are plenty of podcasters who have expensive microphones, compressors, limiters, top-end recording and pro editing software, studio quality monitor speakers for playback, expensive headphones, and a mixer.

You don't need them all to start podcasting. Ultimately, content (what you are talking about) overcomes most things. i.e., if what you are saying is interesting enough, you are engaging in your delivery, and people can understand what you are a saying (i.e; they can hear your voice clearly) then you are basically home and dry. All the rest falls under 'nice to have'.

Plenty of people use the free Audacity recording software www.audacity.sourceforge.net (available for PCs and Macs), or GarageBand (free with a Mac).

Both are fine for recording and editing your shows, to remove mistakes and unwanted noises (if you are so inclined).

Yes, you can spend a lot of money on gear – but will it make the content any more interesting? No it won't. While it may improve the overall technical quality of your podcast (which is great), most listeners won't care too much or judge you on it.

Plenty of people get by using a budget USB microphone plugged into their PC. But have a look around your home and see what microphone you may have to hand. Plug it in, give it a go, and see what you think. Experiment.

I guess I have two key things I want to share in this section:
1) Use what you have, and do it anyway. It is really important that you don't allow a lack of top quality gear to be a barrier to making a podcast
2) Don't spend a lot of money just to start podcasting, because if it does fizzle out in a few months' time (as many do) then you won't have spent a lot of money for little gain

Microphones

There are two types of microphone; condenser and dynamic. For home 'studios' that do not have much in the way of soundproofing or acoustic treatment (to reduce room reverb), I'd always opt for a dynamic microphone.

Dynamic microphones

The Shure SM58 is a popular choice and often used with a pop filter by podcasters. The SM58, like all dynamic microphones, only picks up sound that is right in front of them and are ideal if you happen to have less than an ideal environment in which to record.

Dynamic mics do not need to be powered, but will likely need to be plugged into a mixer to raise the volume. They may not work well plugged straight into a computer (but give it a go).

In my view your first choice should be a dynamic microphone; they may not sound as crisp as a condenser, but they are more forgiving when recording conditions are less than perfect.

Condenser microphones

Condenser microphones are highly sensitive, and can pick up a snail clearing its throat from three miles away.

Condenser mics often deliver a far crisper and richer sound than dynamic mics, but in my opinion, to use a condenser microphone you really need a soundproofed room and acoustic tiles on all flat areas to reduce sound from bouncing off hard surfaces. There's nothing worse than room boom or reverb to ruin an otherwise fine recording.

Condenser microphones also need to be powered, either by a battery inside the mic, or by the mixer/microphone amp they are connected to (via 48 volt phantom power). Not all mixers provide a phantom power option.

USB microphones

USB microphones are well worth considering. These can be plugged directly into the USB socket of your computer and have risen in quality during the last few years.

However, if you use a USB microphone, and plug your headphones into the audio output socket of your computer, you will most likely hear a delay between saying something and hearing it in your headphones. This is down to what's called 'latency' – the speed at which your computer processes incoming sound and sends it back out.

If using a USB microphone, be sure to buy one that features a headphone socket as part of the microphone housing to avoid the latency issue.

The alternative is to use an external mixer that features a headphone socket. So your mic and headphones are both plugged into the mixer, and your mixer's output is plugged into your recording device.

Digital recorder

A digital recorder, which is a few steps up from a dictation recorder, can be ideal and are very versatile, particularly if you need to record an interview while out in the field, at trade shows and other events.

The audio quality of these units is incredible in my opinion, the built-in microphone is fine for most purposes (watch out for wind noise though if recording outside) and most provide an option to plug in an external mic (many units offer 48v phantom power for condenser microphones), as well as a socket for your headphones to monitor the recording.

Once a recording has been completed with an external recorder, the digital file is copied to the computer for post production and final output.

If recording in the field, a shotgun mic can be a good option.

Smartphone

Of course we mustn't forget the smartphone. The built-in microphone (at the bottom of your phone) can be used, although the quality may be a bit below parr.

However, it can be enhanced with software to increase the base and compression can give it a bit of body, the file may also need to be converted to MP3.

There are a number of cables around to help you plug in a quality microphone and a growing number of attachments for some smartphones that will greatly improve your recordings.

Again, these are well worth considering if you need the versatility of recording on the move, perhaps interviewing people at conferences etc.

At their core, smartphones are computers and digital recording devices – their weak spot for recording quality audio is often the built-in microphone or low quality recording format.

Lapel microphone

A lapel microphone (or lavalier) could be an option for you. You'll notice TV newsreaders using them a lot and I have also seen them used at some radio stations too.

These tiny mics do a great job and the price has really come down, some models selling for around $30. But as with everything else, you get what you pay for.

Best for the job

In my view the best microphone is the one that suits your voice and the environment it is used in. There is no point placing a top of the line condenser microphone in a spare room / 'home studio' unless the room is soundproofed and acoustically treated with things such as professional sound dispersing tiles on the walls and ceiling.

Don't get hung up on spending lots of money or following the trend. Do what is right for you and your budget. If the recording sounds good, then it is. End of.

Headphones

Listening to your voice through headphones while you speak means you'll hear any mouth clicks, next door's dog barking, as well as any other noises.

However, plenty of people say that by not wearing headphones you will get a more natural sounding recording. So try recording with and without headphones, play it back to listen, and decide which delivery you are happier with.

My preference is to wear headphones because by actively listening to what I am saying I hear if my diction gets a bit sloppy, hear any un-wanted noises – and can do a retake on the fly and edit out unwanted material later.

You have to listen to your recording at some point, so it may as well be while recording it. If recording outside then using headphones is a must as noises from vehicles and the wind can ruin a recording (it's bet-ter to hear it when it happens and do a retake right away). People will stop listening if they struggle to hear what's being said.

Recording equipment

Most people use their computer to record their podcasts. But a few opt to use a digital recorder. One reason for using an external recorder is that some people have found the soundcard in their computer introduces unwanted noise to their recordings – noise they hadn't heard when playing music.

Having an audio recorder separate from the computer keeps these sound issues out of the way – as well as reduce the risk of 'earth hum'.

Earth hum is often caused by the combination of a computer, mixer, external speakers, and other computer add-ons creating an earth loop – and the humming noise caused by this can be really hard to solve.

I once spent days unplugging cables and power cords to solve an unwanted hum and I never did fix it. Then one day my phone stopped working and an engineer discovered my phone line had a bad earth (it was connected to my mixer for phone interviews) problem solved.

Bottom line, use what works for you and that is hopefully what you already have.

Also consider that each mic has a different sound, and once you start buying microphones, and you are serious about podcasting over a number of years, you will go through a few until you find a mic that is perfect for your voice.

By all means, use what's at hand for now, but try before you buy if it is possible. If a friend has a mic then ask to borrow it and see if it suits your voice.

As your ears become tuned to recording your voice, you'll likely start to become a bit fussy until you find the right mic for you.

Quick tips: Keep a sipper bottle of water with you when recording in the studio to reduce mouth noises. Don't use a glass of water because you *will* spill it over your equipment. Keeping your mouth lubricated and your lips moist will stop lots of mouth clicks.

When recording: TV off, aircon off, windows and doors closed, curtains drawn to help reduce the reverb of your voice as it bounces off hard flat surfaces such as walls, windows and your desk.

Key take away
Podcast with the gear you have and do it anyway.

Going solo

Should you host your podcast on your own, or with a co-host? There are merits in each case. For example, for a techie podcast, one person might be an expert in software, the other an expert in hardware. This is an ideal combination. But two people talking about the same thing from the same perspective with similar views...? I'm not sure where the value-add is for the listener.

Also, if you do team up to podcast with other people then you have to all agree on when and where to record the show. This can lead to people not turning up, not pulling their weight, or being late which can lead to frustration for you, and it can all slip very quickly.

Podcasting with a co-host can also prevent you from finding you have an hour to spare and using that time to record your podcast. For example, at home I might discover the house is quiet and I will take the opportunity to record my podcast. Later when everyone is home and it's noisy I'll edit the show and do post production.

My preference is to go solo, and to perhaps invite on a guest now and then to add a little variety to the proceedings.

There's one other thing to consider too. Should you and your podcast partner have a falling out, or one person moves away (and wants to continue with the podcast at their new location with a new co-host) then who owns the podcast, its format, artwork, brand, goodwill, website, advertising income, email database, rights etc? You or them?

My advice is to nut this out before you start. A written agreement that come the day you part ways – for whatever reason – that you have the right to carry on hosting the show and own all of the above.

In addition, you don't want a former co-host demanding you take down all shows that feature them due to copyright reasons. It's a legal grey area you do not want to enter, it's an area that can be avoided by having everything set out in a signed agreement before episode one is recorded.

> **Key take away**
> Go solo for greater flexibility and invite guests for variety.

Your first podcast

Recording your first podcast is always very exciting. The trick is to keep it simple, and not to over-stretch yourself – don't set yourself up to fail – restrict your podcasting ambitions to what you can reasonably achieve today.

By now you have got your topic sorted, perhaps even decided on a short piece of intro and outro music. You may even have paid for a very short professional podcast intro featuring your name and the name of your podcast.

With your notes ready – use them as a guide, not a script – and the place nice and quiet, sit yourself in front of the mic with a sipper bottle of room temperature water.

Do a little test run to get your mic in the best position and check the audio levels – not too loud, not too quiet. Be sure to record your show in Mono (not stereo).

If you are able to see a visual guide to the recording levels as you speak, try and get them to bounce between minus 12db and minus 6db (–12db to –6db). At this setting, it will give you some headroom should you raise your voice a little. You can make the finished audio -1db in post.

What you don't want is to record your voice at zero db – full volume. Because you risk ending up with sections being distorted – and there is nothing you can do to fix it, apart from recording those sections again. Stay well out of the red zone on your audio meter when recording.

Pop your headphones on, speak, and listen to yourself. Keep an ear out for background noise (such as birds tweeting, the office printer humming, or your computer's fan).

Open your show with a nice warm welcome, tell listeners who you are and what's coming up. Complete your recording and end the show with a request that people subscribe, rate your show, and check out your website for more information (i.e. to read your show notes and join your email list).

Keep a note pad on your desk and if you make a mistake during the recording just jot down the time it happened. So if you trip up at 8 minutes into the recording, write down '8', redo the section you fluffed and carry on with your show. At the end of the recording go back and edit out the errors. You'll either make fewer errors as time goes on or become an expert audio editor.

What to tell listeners in every podcast
- Your name
- The name of your podcast
- Your website address
- Episode number
- What's coming up in this show

If you are covering topical issues you should tell listeners the date because they may listen to it years later. But if you are offering more generic / timeless information then adding a date may not be a good idea as you want your podcasts to sound as fresh as possible, for as long as possible, in which case just use an episode number.

Stating a date or episode number helps listeners ID the edition should they write to you about that episode.

Okay, with your voice recorded, and your first show almost done, save your recording to a folder called Podcasts, and name the recording, I suggest a formula such as: Episode number-Title-Date.WAV (01-WordPress-06July2019.WAV). I write in the month as 0607 could be 6 July or 7 June.

Open your recording up in an audio editor and go over the recording to see if any sections need re–recording, or if you want to chop out any unwanted comments, mumbles or noises.

Once you have the recording just how you like it, use your audio software to normalise the whole recording to -1db. Use your preferred audio editing software to mix in your intro and outro music (if you are using them, they are not compulsory).

Once the show is completed, export it as an MP3 file (64kbps Mono 44.1khz). Now use an ID3 meta tag app to add your artwork to the MP3 file along with meta data etc.

The larger the file size of the artwork attached to your MP3, the larger the file size of your MP3 becomes – so make artwork no larger than needed (i.e.; don't attach high resolution artwork to the MP3 – make a smaller versions of say 100px square at 72dpi and optimise it for the web delivery if you have image software that has that option.

Do a web search for ID3 software, there are some free apps around. Adding meta tag data is essential in my view to clearly display the title information of your show on Podcast players correctly.

With everything done, listen to your podcast one more time all the way through (another reason to keep it short). Happy?

Upload the MP3 to wherever it is you are storing your podcasts, place the MP3's unique URL in the podcast field in a post/page (such as in the Blubbry plugin) on your website, publish, and check to see it appears in your dedicated podcast RSS feed.

You need a dedicated (RSS) feed for podcasts (as you don't want to send text-only posts to podcast streaming services using your site's default feed). The URL of the podcast feed will become apparent once you get started on the journey to podcasting.

I am a huge fan of WordPress and the Blubrry podcast plug in. Both are free so I highly recommend you use these as they really do make sharing your podcast almost idiot proof (I'm living proof of that).

Okay, your first podcast is in the bag, all done, uploaded and free to the world. So with one podcast listed it's time to submit your podcast feed to all the podcast libraries you can. This will take time particularly when preparing custom artwork for each distributor.

It's a good idea to plan shows in advance, because that way you can say during podcast one what is coming up in number two, and so on – you want to promote your next podcast to encourage people to come back next time and subscribe. Subscribers are gold!

Even if your show is news driven, and you don't exactly know what's happening in advance, you may have a regular feature in the show that you can point to (if not, consider having a regular feature).

At the very least your podcast will be on a page on your website which can be shared on all your social media channels. Ask friends and colleagues to share and like it. At this point it is no good being shy. You have done the hard yards, now the slow process of building a following

Interviewing skills

Your podcast may do just fine with you sharing your news and ideas with listeners. But now and again you might want to spice things up and feature a guest on your podcast. If they can sit with you then great.

However, it's likely you'll want to interview someone who can't visit you because they live too far away. Google Hangouts, Zoom and Skype are perfect for recording interviews with people based almost anywhere in the world.

I use Skype with a paid-for add-on from Ecamm (www.ecamm.com) called Skype Recorder. It allows users to record all Skype conversations automatically, and provides a recording that you can split; i.e., you can separate your voice from that of your interviewee's into two separate mono tracks – and that allows you to level off volumes on each track independently and remove unwanted noises that may appear on one side of the conversation, but not the other.

These noises can include people speaking over each other, background noises and connection glitches.

The amount of work you do here depends on how polished you want the end result to be. You can do a short interview and upload it quickly, or spend time editing and processing it to get the best quality you can.

Now, if you buy some credits on Skype you can call people on their mobile and landline phones directly from your Skype app. So if someone you want to interview doesn't have a Skype account, or a reliable/fast internet service, you can call them on their 'normal' phone.

Feel free to experiment with all the options available and do a few test recordings with friends to establish your computer and recording software is all set up and working as expected.

If you want to stick with a traditional landline then there are one or two old-school gadgets still around that will connect your phone line to your mixer.

One advantage of using an old-school phone line is that you can take the audio from the phone into your mixer where you can raise and lower the volume of the phone on the fly. Sometimes I have placed the phone hard right on the stereo image, and my studio mic on hard left (then after editing, mixed the channels into one mono file).

Using a standard phone may mean you speaking into the phone handset and your studio microphone at the same time – unless you send the signal of your microphone/mixer down the phone line for your interviewee to hear you (it can be done).

There are also myriad paid-for services such as conference call providers whereby various people can dial in to talk to each other. Most of these conference call firms will send you an MP3 recording of the conversation, but in my experience the quality is not always ideal for broadcast. Still, it is an option – just not one I have ever used for any podcast I have produced.

In addition there are plenty of apps for smartphones that will record a conversation, and again while these work very well, the quality may not be totally acceptable. Having said that, I have used them once or twice.

I was out shopping when my interviewee called to set a new time for our interview that didn't suit me. So, knowing my phone recorded all calls automatically I said "let's do it now". He agreed and so I interviewed him (I only had four or five questions and so it was all over in 10 minutes). Back home I copied the file across to the computer, enhanced the audio slightly with a bit of bass boost, re-voiced my questions using the studio mic and mixed it altogether. It worked.

You can also run a cable from your mobile phone's headphone socket to the input of your mixer.

Truth is that nowadays there are dozens of options available to record phone calls, so the real questions is – which method will deliver the quality you need along with it being convenient for you to use?

I have settled on Skype as the audio quality is good (I tend to turn off the camera to keep the conversation audio only) and it is easy to use.

Because podcasters will always use domestic solutions to record phone interviews (because we are not talk radio stations) there will always be a trade-off that involves some level of compromise and fixing up afterward (it's this post-production that often takes a lot of time).

But that shouldn't put you off because scoring a good interview with an expert or specialist will help attract listeners and build your profile.

Once you do one interview well, others will follow.

And to be honest, having interesting guests on your podcast really does add value for the listener. A word of warning though, don't get all gushy. Keep it business-like, ask one question at a time and if the interviewee starts rambling, chip in and ask another question – keep it tight.

It is also worth noting that because people's jobs change as they move in and out of different industries (or their opinions change over the years) it is worth saying the date in your podcast – just so future listeners can put it into context.

For example: "I spoke with Jim Smith on 18th June 2019 via Skype to ask him about his findings...". Keep it transparent.

Another good thing is that hopefully your interviewee will share your podcast with their network, and that could give you exposure to a whole new audience and requests from other people to feature on your show.

Prepare for the interview

Having done your research, write down a list of say five to 10 key questions. You may not get to ask them all, as one answer may lead you down another line of questioning (listen to the answers).

Discipline yourself to ask one question at a time. It is far better to ask one question than ramble on asking lots of questions in one go.

Good: What was the purpose of the meeting with Jon Doe?
Not good: I hear you met with Jon Doe...What did you discuss and is it true you didn't get on – I heard your wife was also there. Who else was there?

Do not pretend you know it all. If you hear something that is new information that's relevant to the interview, ask a follow-up question.

Sometimes interviewees will says something such as: "Well of course you'll understand why we made that decision…" Well, no, you may not understand and don't pretend you do if you don't. And even if *you* do – your listeners may not.

Have your interviewee explain it in plain language so we can all understand, don't fall into the trap of trying to appear more informed than you actually are – always have the interviewee explain things in plain language. Ask a question and listen to see if your guest answers it.

Now, few interviews heard in a podcast are confrontational as they normally feature kindred spirits. They are what's called soft interviews, and one reason for that is that a guest would not knowingly agree to being recorded while being asked some uncomfortable questions. But it can be done, and it is something I was able to do when producing my news podcast a few years back. But most of my podcast interviews have been with people I agreed with or was happy to offer exposure to.

So podcasts mainly feature soft interviews for lots of reasons. Chief among them is that – if we are honest – the podcaster is often just pleased to have a guest agree to take part (and I don't mean any disrespect to podcasters by saying that). It can be a bit of a buzz, particularly if the guest has a high profile.

Silence please

Now, there's one interview technique that even some professionals fail to master. The art of silence – even in friendly interviews. Remaining silent is critical when it comes to interviewing someone, so never be afraid of silence.

Ask a question and wait for the person to answer. Do not interrupt them, don't murmur a syllable, do not answer it for them with a multiple choice option, just let them talk – give them some air.

Listen to what they say. Stay focused on the interview, stay in the moment and don't drift off with thoughts of mowing the lawn.

Be ready to move your guest on if they start to wander off topic. Keep listeners in mind throughout. Don't assume anything

If you want to see (hear) a good example of how to manage a radio interview listen to Amy Goodman on DemocracyNow.org. You can learn a lot just by watching how methodically she poses questions, fills in the gaps for listeners, and doesn't take anything for granted on behalf of her audience. Great interviews rely on thoughtful questions and giving the interviewee time to speak without interruption.

How to be a successful interviewer

There are three stages to a successful interview:

- Finding the best person to answer your questions
- Preparing for the interview by doing solid background research
- Conducting the interview by asking insightful questions (don't be a cliché)

Research

Research is needed to find the best people to interview. Facebook, LinkedIn, known contacts, other people's podcasts, and general research will lead you to the right people.

Having found them you sometimes need to jolly them along and encourage them to take part in your podcast. Bottom line, no one is obliged to answer your questions. But the more established your podcast is, the easier it will be. Interviewees and their representatives look for credibility. What can you offer them? And what can they offer you?

On location

Going to visit an interviewee where they work can make for a very interesting interview as you meet the person on their home soil. Face to face interviews are best.

Before you enter their office press record and leave it on until after you leave, you'll pick up the atmosphere of the site such as office noise and machinery. Don't turn your recorder off right at the end of the interview because as soon as the interviewee thinks it is all over they will relax and won't stop talking.

Comments that were recorded when the subject thought the recorder was turned off can't be used without their permission.

As the interview starts let your subject know that you won't be saying much when they speak, so as not to spoil the recording. And put their mind to rest saying the recording will be edited, so any slip ups will be cut out of the final podcast and they are free to 'start over' if they want to answer a question in a different way.

Before you ask any questions, make sure your source is recorded identifying themselves with their name and title they want you to use.

Be careful not to say anything when the person is talking, as we all do naturally in conversation. Just nod your head, smile, and make eye contact to show you are listening.

If you have time, ask a few throwaway questions to start the interview, just to get them used to the situation of a microphone being there.

"How long have you been doing this kind of work?" "How did you get into it?" "Where did you get that tie?"

If you're not sure what to ask, remember that your ignorance can often be an asset. Start with a really general question, such as "What is happening here?", "What are you doing there?". If you run out of questions during the interview, ask, "What's the next step?" It's a great open-ended question and the answer may surprise you and your listeners.

Once the interview is about over, you should always ask: "Is there anything else you'd like to add?"

Recording

Positioning your microphone correctly is essential. When someone sees a mic pointed at them they often clam up, so hold it out of their direct line of sight – not up against the nose. If standing in front of them hold it vertically pointed up toward their chin from your chest. If they are sitting down, keep it off to the side and pointed at their chin.

Always record a few minutes of atmos/room noise (every room sounds different even when it appears to be perfectly silent). You can use this atmos to cover dialogue editing (trust me, you will need it, particularly the day you don't do it).

Headphones will help you correct the most common sound problems such as popping Ps and room reverb etc that cannot be fixed in post production. It may seem silly wearing headphones while interviewing someone, but I highly recommend it. It may just save you having to ask to do the interview again (amateur week).

Public relation firms

You may need to contact a PR firm to set up an interview. Now, these guys are not necessarily there to help you – they are paid to help their client. But if you do call one, never agree to send them your questions in advance. Just never ever do it (no matter what they say).

"Oh, everyone else sends us their questions as it helps us prepare better answers." You don't want 'better answers' you want unrehearsed answers that sound natural – not set pieces read from a script.

My preference is to always go straight to the person I want to interview. Email them, guess their email address if you have to, call them, go knock on their door.

Just don't rely on a PR firm to act in your best interest or in a timely manner because they are brilliant at slowing things down to suit themselves. Don't assume your request will even be passed on to your prospect. Some PR firms make decisions on behalf of their client and only tell them what they think their client needs to know.

So treat with caution, PR people can't afford to be embarrassed for fear of losing the client's business. They are more interested in staying in business than hooking their clients up with risky unknowns.

A word to the wise
Having worked as a journalist for so long I have heard it all.
1) Can I hear the recording before you publish it?
2) Can I see the questions first?
3) Can my lawyer / manager / partner hear it first to fact check it?
4) Can you remove the podcast from your website because...

When requests such as these come in you will have to make a decision on what to do. I wouldn't agree to items 1, 2 and 3 as you are basically handing over editorial control to someone else and suddenly you find you are making the podcast to suit your interviewee (I assume they haven't paid to appear on your podcast).

Being asked to take down a podcast brings on a sinking feeling. But the podcast is out there and it has been heard and downloaded by who knows how many people. Find out what the big issue is and maybe a short re-edit can solve it to everyone's satisfaction. But deal in matters of fact, not opinion.

Fact: "I said three when I meant 33". (better fix that)
Opinion: "My partner says the podcast makes me sound silly". (con-

vince them otherwise).

You may be faced with moral and ethical issues and you have to decide how to respond. You are in the media now and face all the pitfalls that come with it (see the section on media law).

Your interview should be as entertaining as possible, flow and be engaging. If you get bored listening to it, then so will your listeners.

Top tips

- Interviewing someone you don't know over the phone can feel a bit awkward, particularly if you are both new to this game. In which case put the other party at ease by reminding them that if they make a mistake or want to start over, then all they need do is say so because you are not aiming to embarrass anyone and you want the best show possible
- And because you can't see each other, two people speaking at the same time is common – particularly if there is a bit of a delay on the line. So ask your question and wait for the answer
- Ask one open-ended question at a time
- Decide whether you want a conversational interview or a strict question and answer
- Record everything
- Editing software allows you to easily slice up sentences to have them mean something quite different to what was intended. You can't do this

Key take away
Research, ask clear questions, and let your guest fill the silence.

Popular gadgets such as this take an audio feed from a landline phone to your mixer. You will need to speak into the phone handset for your interviewee to hear your questions and speak into your studio mic at the same time or re-record your questions later.

Mixer set up

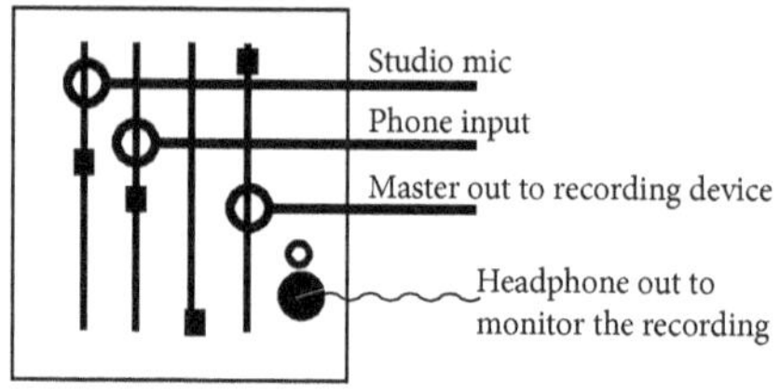

Use a smartphone as a combined mic and recorder, or for phone interviews just plug a cable into its socket and connect it to the input of your mixer. Another option is to install an app that records calls (set it to highest quality recording).

Services such as Skype, Zoom, Google Hangouts...Will allow you to record conversations that pass through your computer or smartphone over the internet.

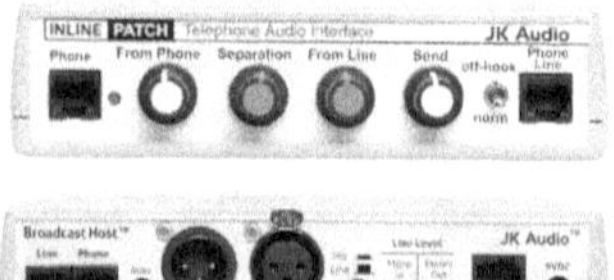

The JK Audio Broadcast Host Desktop Digital Hybrid will feed a call into your mixer from a standard phone line and send your mixer's output down the phone line to your guest.

Artwork

If you have looked through any podcast library you will have seen all the logos associated with every podcast. Depending on how artistic you are, you may be able to create something quite nice (but a bit of professional help may be needed for this one-off item that will be with you for the life of your podcast).

If you already have a company, and your podcast is associated with it, then half the work may already be done. You may already have the colours sorted and an icon/logo designed. Now you just need to reformat it into a podcast logo.

Every podcast library will need a logo supplied to their specifications. There is no one-size fits all podcast artwork.

The thing about logos is that they need to work at most any size. From tiny icon upwards – and this needs to be fully considered from the outset when thinking of your design.

Look at chains such as McDonalds or BurgerKing for example, or BP and Shell. Each firm uses common colours and simple shapes. I can assure you hundreds of thousands of dollars were spent nailing down every tiny aspect of the logos used by corporations. Look and learn.

Colours are important. For example, a high quality jeweller wouldn't use the colour orange (too brash). A fast food 'restaurant' wouldn't use blue and green, those colours are often used by banks.

I recommend you do a search on the psychology of colours to find which colours work for the subject matter of your podcast and settle on a maximum of two colours plus black or white.

One book I often refer to is *Guide to Communicating with Color* by Leatrice Eiseman (ISBN: 0-9666383-2-8). It's well worth reading if you can get a copy, but there are of course plenty of websites offering similar information.

Colours send out signals to people, so the colours you choose need to be in keeping with your brand and subject matter.

The trick with your logo is for it not to be too complex. Simplify, simplify, simplify. For every design decision you make, ask yourself 'why'.

Why this colour, why this shape, why these words, why this font?

Once you decide what colour and typefaces (fonts) you are adopting you need to stick with them and use them on your website, business card, social media logos... Everywhere. That's how brands are built. Not by using different colours or different fonts every time you go to brand something associated with your podcast.

Another reason for having a logo is that the people at Apple etc may give you a bit more prominence if you have cool podcast artwork.

And the more eye-catching it is, the more likely someone browsing a podcast library will click on it.

Confused about where to start? Have a look at other people's podcast artwork and decide which style appeals to you, and then emulate their look and feel when creating your artwork, but don't copy it wholesale.

Each podcatcher – Apple, Spreaker, TuneIn, Stitcher etc – will have their own specifications for your show's artwork.

Not only do you need to send them your logo at the required size and resolution, but your logo needs to be flexible enough to be altered to the optimal shape. For example, some firms require square others want oblong.

So ensure your artwork is flexible so it can be adjusted to different shapes, while remaining consistent. Check out all the logo specification requirements of the podcast libraries you want to be listed in.

Colours essentially come in two varieties; CMYK for printing and RGB for everything else. CMYK stands for Cyan, Magenta, Yellow and Keyline (which is Black).

Under the RGB banner of Red, Green and Blue hide a huge range of Web only colours. These are called Hexadecimal (Hex) colours and are made up of six letters and numbers; such as 000000 (which is black).

The reason I mention this is because once you get your logo back from your designer it would be handy if they told you specifically which colours were used.

Then you can easily alter your website's colours by adopting the Hex pallet associated with your logo. Consistency is key. People will see your logo, click through to your website and recognise the colours. It links everything together in the subconscious and looks professional.

My real estate podcast artwork featured a handsome chap and a silhouette of Auckland city. Using a silhouette avoided showing companies' buildings.

As you can see, I followed a similar format for my WordPress podcast. I used my website URL.

The letters in grey are really red; but you get the general idea. This was a one hour weekly news, music, and interview podcast.

I'd probably do this artwork differently now, but this was an early podcast linked to my job writing about careers and training.

Key take away
When it comes to artwork; use appropriate colours and simplify, simplify, simplify.

Hosting and storage

For people to play and download your podcasts, you need to have your MP3s stored online somewhere – in the 'cloud'. Once this has been arranged you can get a unique RSS feed (URL/web link) just for your podcast episodes.

The RSS feed is submitted to distributors such as Apple, Spreaker, Stitcher, TuneIn, and other podcast libraries that will use this link to present your podcasts to their visitors.

The benefit of having your MP3s hosted by a third party (such as Libsyn or Blubrry etc) is that you get an RSS feed that is independent of your website and means you do not need a website to share your podcasts.

However, there are plenty of podcasters who upload their MP3 files to a folder on their own website hosting plan (where their website pages/files are stored). And this is OK – to a point. Problems can arise if you want to close your website down because you have stopped doing new episodes of your podcast, but want to keep your old episodes accessible to the podcast libraries. This is where having an independent RSS feed is like gold (it can save an awful lot of headaches).

Other benefits of hosting your MP3s with a podcasting company is that they should provide fast download speeds of your podcasts to listeners and ideally have their own audio player that can be placed (embedded) on any website page using a simple HTML code.

As mentioned earlier, I am a big fan of WordPress (self hosted) and the Blubrry podcast plugin. The plugin provides everything you need to feature the podcast on your WordPress site and share it with the major podcast libraries.

I recommend you research your options and perhaps try out a few podcast plugins before settling on the one that best suits you.

So you have a decision to make. Host your podcast on a third party site, or store the MP3s in the same place as your own website (assuming you have one) – in which case you'll need to have enough space to store your files and enough bandwidth to cope with demand.

Remember, most hosting plans have limits on both storage and monthly bandwidth use. It's now time for some math...Imagine one podcast is 5meg in size and 400 people download it in one month, that will take two gigs of bandwidth (2Gig). You need to work out if the bandwidth allocation of your hosting plan will be enough. Because if you use up your monthly bandwidth allowance, your website won't load and your emails will stop too. Ideally you will have an unlimited hosting plan.

To store MP3s on your website hosting plan you'll need an FTP app to access the place where your website pages are stored. Once there, create a new folder, name it (podcasts), and upload your podcast and show artwork. This folder will have a unique URL, use it to 'tell' your podcast plugin where to find your podcasts – you'll paste the URL somewhere in the admin area of your website or the plug-in's control panel (all will become apparent and fall into place as you step through the procedure in real life). Your URL will look something like this; www.yourwebsite.com/podcasts/

Shared website hosting plans, which is what most people have, aren't always ideal for mass downloads, and some hosting firms get a bit tetchy about their servers being 'abused'.

If your podcast starts getting too popular – with downloads in their thousands every week – you will likely need to have the MP3 files hosted by a podcast hosting firm so your listeners get faster and more reliable downloads (and their popularity doesn't bring your website and business to its knees).

Dedicated website

Talking of hosting, unless the podcast is directly linked to a website you already have, it is worth buying the domain name of your podcast and creating a website specifically for it. It can really help market and develop the brand when people search for it by name.

A dedicated website helps people find you, provides a clear point of contact for listener feedback and for people to send you information that may be of interest to you and your listeners.

For the uninitiated, there are two elements to every website. The domain name or URL, i.e. *www.SteveHart.co.nz* and the hosting services where your website pages and files are stored – you need to pay for both. A web domain name is about $20 a year and expect to pay around $150 for professional website hosting. On top of this is the cost of website design and any ongoing maintenance if you are unable to do it yourself.

The files that make up a website have to be stored by a web hosting company so people can see your website when they type in your URL / domain name or search for you.

If you are serious about your podcast, buy the domain name for it (before someone else does). And of course there are hundreds of suffix options nowadays, from the common dot Com to dot Asia, dot photography and others. It can get very expensive buying up all relevant domain suffixes, so do what's right for you.

Another benefit of having a dedicated website is that you can place adverts on it (Google and Amazon for example) and cross promote your other businesses on it.

You can create a profile page for yourself and a contact form.

A well-designed (smartphone compatible) website adds credibility to your podcast, shows you are serious about it, and can include a list of all your shows with photos of guests, shownotes and videos etc.

Key take away
Having done the podcast, make sure people can easily find it online.

Show notes

Notes about each podcast you produce are essential. These show notes go on your website – on the same page as your podcast audio player – one post for each podcast episode.

The purpose of these show notes is to not only let readers know what's in the podcast if they visit your website, but for search engines to index your pages in their databases.

So if someone searches for something you have covered in a podcast, they will find it via the text on your website, and then happen upon your podcast.

Comprehensive and SEO keyworded show notes are a must (and these keywords should also feature in the meta data of your MP3s).

Writing show notes should reflect the content of the podcast and expand on the theme as well. Your show notes can feature added content as well as links to websites mentioned.

In my WordPress podcast I will talk about a certain plugin and then direct listeners to my website for show notes and links that allow them to click straight through to the plugins mentioned, so they can be downloaded from the originator's website.

Remember also that some people may not be able to listen to your podcast right away and so may enjoy reading your show notes. They may also share them with friends and colleagues on social media.

Show notes can also be translated easily into other languages using one of many online apps, so your information can be accessible to people who speak a different language to you.

While the podcast is obviously the key to this little book, my emphasis on writing comprehensive show notes needs to be taken on board as they add real value to your podcast, website and profile.

Your show notes might even be the basis of a press release. So build on them every week to make a press release and send it to all the press release distribution sites you can – not forgetting relevant trade websites, local news sites, anywhere you can (build an email list of media outlets that may be interested in your podcast). All media outlets are looking for content, and while your press release may not make the cut this week, it may well be just what someone needs next week.

It is fair to say that not every podcaster or business owner is a brilliant writer, so when it comes to show notes and press releases etc, you may need to draw on the writing skills of a colleague or a professional writer with experience of writing for news outlets.

What you can't afford to do is allow poor spelling, grammar or substandard sentence construction to confuse the story flow and lower your reputation.

If you think you need help writing show notes, then ask for it – because there's nothing worse than a business website littered with mistakes (it's not a good look).

Speech to text

Writing comprehensive show notes can take a lot of time, as you listen to the recording and type what's being said.

Thankfully, there are a growing number of free online options to help you. Search for speech to text services and you will find websites where you can upload your MP3 for its AI system to 'listen' to your audio and do its best to transcribe what's said into a text document you can download.

Some are better than others, and none currently will transcribe perfectly. But if you want to save yourself hours of typing, and are happy to check over the text documents, then you may save a lot of time.

Search Engine Optimization

SEO is the practice of using key words in your show notes in a fluid way that doesn't jar the reader. You need to flow in words that relate to your podcast/business and which your customers may use in a search engine to find the things you offer.

Make a list of the key words you need to include...It's a case of guesswork, science, and experience.

There's always a bigger fish

Chances are you will not be the first person to podcast about your chosen topic. And just because someone may already be doing something similar that doesn't mean you should not go ahead and do your own thing – far from it.

No matter what the subject matter, you will bring your own style and twist to it. And while one listener may not enjoy the other podcaster's take on the subject, or their voice / delivery style etc, they may enjoy yours.

Sure, there may be some cross-over on the topics you and other podcasters cover, but so what? And as we all know, podcasts do come and go. So who's to say that any existing podcasts will be around next week – they may be about to pull the plug on their show, and then in you come to fill the void.

It is a good idea to listen to how other podcasts in your arena cover and report on the subject. They may mention things you were not aware of, or you may find a gap in what they are talking about and then cover that in your podcast.

Everyone has a voice, everyone is different, everyone looks at news and issues from their own perspective and uses that information in their own way.

Let's face it, most podcasts offer opinions on the subject at hand. So and so company has brought out a new gadget at $99 each (facts). Now here's your opinion – it's that opinion, and the way it is delivered that makes you different to the other guy.

So don't look at yourself as coming second, third or forth to other podcasters. See yourself as number one among a collective of podcasters with similar interests or hobbies. Build your own audience and perhaps interview other podcasters on your show for cross promotion. I find most podcasters to be quite supportive of each other.

Key take away
You may not be first, but you can better and different.

Promotion

If the whole purpose of your podcast is to drum up business, then you need to make direct contact with your listeners. Now, you won't know who in the world is downloading your podcasts, so you need listeners to visit your website, sign up to receive emails from you and hopefully buy something.

You can offer to send subscribers additional industry tips and information, as well as an email every time you publish a new podcast – using what's called an RSS driven email campaign via mass-mail companies such as MailChimp.com or Aweber.com for example. I use MailChimp.com (at the time of writing it's free if you have fewer than 1000 subscribers).

The email address of subscribers is gold. By definition they are interested in you, your firm and its products, so you can market to them directly. Have a special offer / call to action with every podcast email sent out.

In addition, you want to promote every podcast you make across all relevant social media platforms – this can often be automated. So when you publish a post featuring a podcast on your website it is automatically sent to your social media networks. You may even go as far as creating a dedicated page for your podcast on all your social media channels.

This all takes time to set up and is all part of the groundwork of launching a successful podcast, but once it's all done it should look after itself.

Be sure to promote your podcast within relevant industry groups on LinkedIn and Facebook. Search them out, become a member and then post your podcasts for fellow industry professionals to enjoy.

Encourage listeners to follow you on all your social media channels and to join you on your social media pages etc.

Don't forget YouTube. This is a place that's featuring more podcasts than ever before. Some podcasters use a static picture with their podcast video and upload it manually. But, at the time of writing, Spreaker.com (among others) can automate this for you.

You will need to link your YouTube account to your Spreaker account. When you upload an audio only podcast to your Spreaker account it can automatically upload it to your YouTube account featuring a Spreaker logo as the image.

If you want a custom image used instead you will need to create the video yourself, export it and upload it to YouTube manually. But do a search for 'podcast conversion to YouTube' as there are some third party services that will also do this.

Leave no stone unturned in promoting every podcast you make, and be sure to really 'sell' your podcast when promoting it in writing: "In this week's podcast, I cover how to build 10 websites in 10 minutes – the easy way."

Add the URL to your podcast in your email signature [and the email signatures of your staff] so it is really easy for people to go straight to your shows.

If you interview someone, have them link to the podcast from their website, and ask them mention it on their social networks.

You can also market your podcast to the hundreds of internet radio stations – whose owners are always looking for free content. Check out the forums at www.internet-radio.com/community/ and let everyone know that your podcast is available for free rebroadcast.

There may also be companies or trade organisations that will welcome having your podcast on their website.

Key take away
Use every avenue available to promote your podcast.

Podcasting for profit

Making money as a direct result of podcasting is hard; most people podcast to promote or market themselves or their products.
But if you're keen there are two basic revenue streams: charging listeners for access to your podcasts or charging advertisers to appear or be mentioned in your shows.

The fact is that there is so much free content available that few people will pay to listen to a podcast (or even buy a newspaper!). So charging people to listen to them is *almost* a non-starter – but not beyond the realms of possibility if the information is of good quality, unique, and of a highly specialist nature that is near impossible to get elsewhere; or offers some form of training or education (such as learning a language).

And in these cases, the full podcasts would be restricted to only appearing on your website and be behind a members-only paywall. Although you could place an excerpt of each podcast episode on all the normal platforms by way of a promotional teaser, to hook people in and encourage them to visit your site for the full version (or start a free trial) and join your EDM (email newsletter).

But if you are famous or have a high profile and can command a fee for your thoughts and entertainment then that may put you in a different league. For example, comedian Mark Moran has done brilliantly well with his WTF podcast and serves as a good illustration of what can be achieved with dedication, talent and originality (and some high profile guests). He promotes products in his shows and his older podcasts are behind a paywall (the best of both worlds).

So obtaining an income as a direct result of podcasting is not impossible. If it were, companies in the US would not have spent the best part of $479 million on podcast advertising in 2018 (according to IAB's June 2019 report). Remember, the $479m figure only covers North America.

The firm's Podcast Advertising Revenue Study, conducted by PwC US, reveals that advertising in podcasts has risen 53 percent since 2017 and predicts US$1 billion will be spent within North America by firms advertising in podcasts by 2021.

Podcasting is on the up and up, rising 7% in the US during 2018, as people search out credible information from independent sources and those with proven specialist knowledge.

Mark McCrery, CEO of Authentic and Podtrac says: "The tremendous growth in podcast ad spending is further evidence that podcasts continue to deliver strong results for both brand and direct response advertisers.

"Spending by content category also maps closely to the podcast categories with the largest audiences, and with more and more places to discover podcasts, the medium is on a strong growth path."

It's interesting to look at the genres of podcasts that attracted the biggest support from US advertisers and sponsors in 2018.

1.   News/politics/current events at 18.4% (up 38.3% on 2017)
2.   Comedy: 13.9% (up 31.1% on 2017)
3.   Business: 12.8% (up 15.3% on 2017)
4.   Education: 10.6% (up 10.4% on 2017)
5.   Arts & entertainment 10% (down 40.8% on 2017)

The categories above captured more than 65% of all podcast ad revenue in the US.

Revenue for other categories are: True crime (9.1% up 26.4%); Technology (8.8% down 39.7%); Lifestyle (7.3% up 17.7%); Scripted fiction (4% up 344%); Games & hobbies (3.4% up 385%); children's programming (0.6% up 500%); Sports (1% down 73%); Health & medicine (0% down 100% on 2017's 3.8%). That last result, zero ad spend on health & medicine podcasts in the US in 2018 is a surprising result given its free market health care system. Perhaps the majority of healthcare podcasts are of an alternative nature that big pharma wouldn't support.

I'd also say that the 38% rise in revenue for news podcasts is likely due to mainstream media – newspapers and radio – launching their own podcasts with the infrastructure and relationships already in place to pull in advertisers to support them.

According to the 2019 IAB report, cost per thousand is the dominant method for revenue; i.e; podcasters are paid a certain amount per 1000 downloads of a single podcast episode. This means podcasters need a robust system for counting downloads. Stats are money.

Edison Research (www.edisonresearch.com) carried out a survey in the US to establish how popular podcasts were. Among its findings were that marketing to podcast listeners is increasing. It says podcast listeners tend to be "intelligent, have high disposable income, and are open to new ideas".

So how does one make money from free-to-air podcasting?

Well the CPM method is popular when it comes to setting the payment rate. CPM stands for cents per mille; mille is a Latin word meaning thousand (not an incorrect spelling of a long walk home).

The good news is that there is no set rate for the CPM, but the typical average (based on my research) starts at around USD$15 for every 1000 downloads. So if your podcast is downloaded 10,000 times during the agreed CPM period then you get a payment of $150 (less deduction for tax etc).

However; I have heard of people earning $2 per 1000 to $50-plus. The rate you get is the one you agree with an advertiser.

Here's my opinion based on a couple of shoot from the lip examples based on a lifetime in the media (and a bit of guesswork). If a podcast is about buying real estate and an advertiser selling chewing gum comes along then I would not expect to be offered great rates. Where's the relevance for the product to the listener?

However, if a home insurance, conveyancer, or mortgage broker wanted to advertise then I would expect them to pay a very fair rate to promote their services to people who are likely to use their services.

The download period for counting the CPM can range from 30 to 90 days. After which you would be within your rights to re-upload the podcast without the advert being featured.

You'd need a written contract of course and absolutely transparent download stats data from a reputable firm (such as Blubrry which is among those who are IAB certified – www.iab.com – so podcast download numbers are recognised and trusted by advertisers).

Without robust and trusted download numbers you can't hope to achieve the best advertising rates, or even be considered as a credible option by an advertiser who will expect a good return on their investment in your show. So with that out of the way, what are your options?

1) You could consider charging people to appear on your show and be 'interviewed' by you.

This falls under the advertisement-feature / branded content type scenario, where someone comes on your show as a 'special guest', talks about their business and product in a conversational way (but are really expecting to generate business for their company).

While this needs to be made clear to your listeners, most will pick up on this as questions will be soft, supportive of the interviewee's business and the 'special guest' will get to talk up their products while mentioning their website and contact details.

But don't abuse the listener, because they are smart. And if the feature is blatant smack-in-the-face advertising they will turn off and never return. It is a balancing act whereby the guest has to give something away that will be of real use/interest to your listeners while building credibility and ultimately encouraging listeners to visit their website etc.

The best advertising is when you identify a problem your listeners may have and provide a worthwhile, realistic, and affordable solution.

2) Commercial spots: Approach potential advertisers that are in line with your podcast genre/content. For example, maybe you host a podcast about growing food; you'd contact a garden centre to advertise (not an accountancy firm).

In my view any advert lasting longer than 60 seconds risks turning listeners off. According to the IAB survey, 30s to 60s ads are the most popular. It may be because ad buyers insist on that duration (perhaps preferring to use an existing radio ad).

My view is that if you can get an ad down to 10 seconds then the audience will be a lot more forgiving, and that will have a better result for the advertiser and you.

So commercials are ideally short, sweet, and – more importantly – relevant to your audience. Ads also need to work in harmony with your podcast. You can't go from soft chit chat and cut to an ear-piercing commercial that blast away your listeners.

3) Paid spoken endorsement: If you are paid to talk about an advertiser's product by way of personal endorsement then this has been shown to cut through far more than a traditional radio ad. Keep it light, real and chatty – make it flow into the show naturally.
For example: "What a weekend it's been...Out with the kids and so busy I'm exhausted today – thankfully I've got a pot of Joe's Coffee on the go so I think we're all set...Jo's Coffee; look for it where ever you shop."

4) Website ads: This is where you place adverts on your website in the hope a visitor or 20,000 will click one and earn you a few cents. Google ads are popular of course, but the pay rates are low. Amazon is another option, you can feature selected products from the Amazon store on your website and earn money when someone buys a product via your website.

This can work well if talking about a movie or book etc (or even having the author etc on your show to talk about it). You can ask listeners to support your podcast by buying goods via your website. Affiliate schemes also fall under this category.

5) Online store: Drop shipping is also an option for making money from your podcast website and this may be worth exploring. Many drop shipping schemes are promoted as easy money; but rest assured they require dedicated on-going marketing (fine if that's the purpose of your podcast). There will also be a monthly cost to factor in to be a member of such a scheme. Proceed with caution.

6) Donations: One or two people may click your PayPal donate button if you put one on your website, but to be honest, most people will listen to your podcast without visiting your website.

7) Of all the ways to make money, show sponsorship is probably the easiest way. "This week's show is brought to you curtesy of XYZ company..."

Sponsorship is less invasive and distracting for the listener who won't see themselves as being sold to when they hear the sponsorship announcement.

8) Encourage visitors to join your email list and then place product offers in your weekly podcast promo email.

A big selling point is that any commercial in a podcast that's been downloaded will be a part of the recording forever.

So unlike a commercial on radio that is broadcast and gone forever, a commercial in a podcast not only sticks with it, but if the commercial is appropriate for your audience it will resonate with a higher percentage of listeners than a one-size fits all radio station.

However, you need to be careful about limited time offers. Be sure to state a closing date (with the year) for any offers so listeners are not disappointed when they expect a free gift years after the advertising campaign ended.

Types of ads
- Pre-roll: An ad that runs just before your podcast intro starts
- Mid-roll: Does what it says, an ad bang in the middle of your show
- Outro: An ad right at the end of your show
- Offer code or direct response: This will be a discount code unique to your show so the advertiser can measure how many times it is used by your listeners
- CPM rate: Cost per mille (thousand) downloads
- CPA rate: Cost per acquisition. The cost of getting a new customer as a result of an ad on your show

Advertisecast states the following
- 30 second ad (CPM) US$22 to $29
- 60 second ad (CPM) US$27 to $30

Full ad rates guide at: advertisecast.com/podcast-advertising-rates

While it's a great boost to the ego to be approached by advertisers my view is that the time and effort of supplying stats, agreeing a deal and following up afterward to get paid really does have to be worthwhile.

So decide how much you would be happy with to enter an agreement and have it be worth your time and effort, and don't be afraid to, ever so politely, turn potential clients away – they may come back with a better offer.

You can always get creative and agree on the best ad rate you can and then add on (pre-agreed) admin, production costs, script checking... based on a fixed fee or hourly rate.

The cost of the advert is the cost to your client of reaching potential customers – it doesn't cover your time to make it happen and mop everything up afterwards. You may not get paid until 4 months after the ad has run. But if you get booked for multiple shows; then you could be onto something.

Be aware also that most advertisers will be global corporates as your podcast will likely be downloaded by people right across the planet. So Tom's Takeaway down the street likely won't get much value from advertising on your podcast.

And just to sidetrack for a moment; hyperlocal media is growing. Hyperlocal media are newspapers, websites, low power and internet 'radio' stations (and podcasts) that only report on things happening in the local neighbourhood. Perhaps there is some scope for you there; a hyperlocal podcast would be great for people who can't read for whatever reason.

The risk of accepting advertising / sponsorship money is that it can influence your content. For example, would you say a firm is releasing unreliable software or questionable products, if they advertise with you?

What you can't afford to do is break the trust of your listeners. Accepting advertising money may mean that one day you have to make a decision to take the money or follow your ethical compass.

Key take away
Ad revenue is down to having big download numbers and robust stats

Hiring an editor

Not every wannabe-podcaster has the skill to do everything they need to produce a podcast, build a website and write show notes etc. There's no doubt there is a lot more to making a podcast than meets the eye – even if we put to one side that most of us are recording in less than ideal conditions (most podcasts are made in a home office/bedroom, not a fully-equipped studio).

It may mean you need to hire people to help you; either to get you up and running, or with every podcast you make.

I know plenty of people who record their podcast and then send the raw recording to a freelancer to be polished up, and made ready for uploading to the hosting company.

There are freelancers who will do all the heavy lifting for you. From transcribing the podcast, to making comprehensive show notes, to creating podcast posts and uploading files left, right and centre.

Or maybe you just don't have the time, and having done the math you figure it is more economical to out-source some of the work, leaving you free to get on with your life / business.

Before commissioning a freelancer to help you, decide what you can do for yourself and what you want your hired help to do for you. Draw up a list for the freelancer to follow, ideally in the order in which the tasks need to be done. Then of course agree a fee and payment schedule.

You'll likely need to create a login to your website and hosting company.

Writing from the freelancer side of the fence I can say that I have been sent all sorts of files for podcast editing. Some have been recorded really well, others required a lot of work to get them to a point where I was happy the end result reflected my professional values.

It takes the freelancer longer to edit files than it does the person who recorded them. The reason for this is that the freelancer needs to listen to the whole recording, and then go back over it to clean it up and work their magic.

Expect a freelancer to take twice as long as you to edit your work.

Of course the freelancer wants the end result to sound brilliant so that they get the job next week. Because of this they may spend more time on the job than you expect.

Most freelancers bill by the hour or per finished minute, but if your podcast is the same duration every week then you may be able to agree a fixed fee.

Asking a post-production freelancer to reduce the duration of your podcast may be risky. I was once asked to cut the length of a podcast and so I cut out what I thought was superfluous information. The client had different ideas when he heard my edited version of his podcast, so I had to put the section back in and cut something else – the client wasn't able to give me any real direction: "I'll leave it to you...". Dangerous.

What should have been a quick spit and polish job turned into a marathon of sharing the file back and fourth until the client was happy.

If you need sections edited out, either do it yourself or give the editor crystal clear instructions.

It takes time to build up a relationship when it comes to working with new people but if you find a freelancer who 'gets you' and delivers quality work on time then they can be worth their weight.

My best advice for finding people to help you is personal recommendation, ask around and find out who colleagues and associates use. You need someone with a track record of quality work and experience in the industry. Trust is paramount.

The great thing is that there is a world of help available, and people working in different time zones who can get work completed and delivered back in time for breakfast.

Bottom line, you do not need to know it all, because there are some fine people around who can fill the gaps in your skill set.

Working as a podcast producer

As podcasts have become more popular, so small business owners and corporates without any interest in the production of them seek out brilliant people like you to help them market their goods via the medium.

They want to be in the podcasting space, but don't know how, can't be asked, and will pay for your help.

This can be a lucrative avenue for those with the time and gear to provide these services. And to be honest; you don't need too much gear to do this. There are three main ways this can work for the entrepreneur podcast producer.

You the host
Your client may not be comfortable, or have the time, to sit down and record a podcast all by themselves – followed by hours of post production. But they might be happy paying you to 'interview' them and fully produce the podcast. Like a writer being hired to write a press release.

This is how it works. Every week (ideally) you get sent a topic and a list of questions to ask the CEO or some such noteworthy person at the client's office.

You rock up and interview them with a decent mic, digital recorder and headphones; they answer the questions and you edit up the show.

I imagine something like this:

"Welcome to the XYZ company podcast with me Your Name.

"This week Joe Blow of XYZ's new production facility in New Town gave me an exclusive insight into the firm's latest product line. In a sit-down interview he explained why XYZ's widgets are a step up from the competition's....

"So Joe, what makes your widgets different...?"

You can see how some firms might really like this way of marketing their company and its products. They set the agenda, set the questions, give the answers, and sign off the completed recording before it is distributed (by them). A Q&A can make for an interesting way to deliver information.

You the coach

There will be plenty of business owners who fancy the idea of hosting a podcast; they have the time, the confidence, but lack the equipment and expertise to pull it off.

Here you might again rock up armed with a bag of gear and coach the client on how to deliver their podcast using your gear in their office.

You'd talk through what it is they want to say, sit with them as they record it, offer advice and guidance to keep them focused and out of trouble (such as slamming the competition), and ensure that when they've finished recording you have something usable to work with.

Then you edit, polish and send it back for review. So you are offering expert guidance, coaching, gear hire, and full post production.

Post production

Offering post production services might well be the easier out of the three... In this case you receive a file featuring the raw podcast for you to edit to perfection; to clean up / remove unwanted noises, coughs, erms and ahs, and level off the volume so it is consistent throughout.

You add intro and outro music, add meta data to the MP3 and you may even upload the MP3 to your client's hosting account (after it has been signed off for release). Plus there's show notes to write. It's a job you can do from anywhere in the world.

Billing

If this is your first time in business then you need to understand what you should be billing for. You also need a separate bank account for this income and to keep accurate tax records (which is a whole other book).

But do charge for: Your time, travel, and agreed expenses (parking, phone calls...). Some people bill by the hour or part thereof, others bill per 15 minutes, some per finished minute of the podcast, or a fixed fee.

The bottom line is that your time, gear, and expertise has real value. Do not sell yourself short, do charge appropriately, and do make a profit. I recommend you attend a small business course to understand your liabilities and how to bill correctly (include tax, sick pay, holidays, etc).

Media Law (if in doubt, leave it out)

I am not a lawyer and cannot offer legal advice. I can only hint at the risks you face when becoming a member of the media – which is what you become as soon as you start publishing words, audio, video and pictures (even if it's just for fun on social media).

And I can assure you that what may seem innocent to you can be a meal ticket for anyone who is offended by what you publish and hires a lawyer to 'put you on notice' that their client seeks 'full redress under all applicable laws'.

Lawyers also like to look after their colleagues and so will often advise you in their first shot across your bows to obtain legal representation at your earliest opportunity.

As a podcaster you need to watch out for slander, defamation and libel. And if those words don't have you running to the toilet, a lawyers' letter threatening to take everything you own may cost you a lorry load of loo paper.

Think the person you talked about in derogatory terms won't hear it? Some lawyers hire agencies to search for potentially libellous, defamatory and slanderous statements and then approach the person named to let them know that they may be able to sue for damages (and they know just the person to do it – no win, no fee).

While being 'right' in what you say is a defence in law, proving it can be time consuming, and actually getting to the steps of the courthouse to present your case before a judge and jury may ruin you in legal fees (expect to pay these up-front). Having said that, most cases are settled out of court with an apology and money changing hands. It's always about the money honey.

It's not quick like the TV shows either with some cases dragging on for years (think McLibel in the UK which ran for 10 years!).

In my opinion, law has little to do with being wrong or right. The winner normally has the strongest resources. And the stress of a court case can really throw you off your game.

You run a risk of legal trouble if you make any statement that harms a person's reputation or makes an 'ordinary' person think less of any person, group or company. These statements include suggesting someone is:

- Guilty of a crime (when they aren't)
- Has behaved improperly
- Calling people dishonest, a liar, a coward, a drunk, saying they have low morals
- Saying that a person, firm or company is in financial difficulty or bankrupt (when they are not)
- Calling someone incompetent or unfit for their job
- Making someone look ridiculous
- Saying anything that could make other people avoid or even pity them – such as, they are insane or have an infectious disease
- You can defame someone even when you don't mention their name if listeners can guess who you mean
- You can defame someone even when what you are saying is true

In order to establish that a person has been defamed they must establish that:

- A statement was published (this includes words in print, on a website, a podcast, social media post – you name it)
- The statement was derogatory of them
- They were identified (they don't need to be named)

Quick note: In Australia companies with more than 10 employees cannot sue for defamation (source; Bell Gully)

How do you know if a statement is defamatory?

The test is objective; so the circumstances under which the words were published can be taken into account, but:

- The person reading/hearing the words are deemed to be of ordinary intelligence with general knowledge and have experience of worldly affairs
- What matters is the meaning to the 'ordinary' person
- An ordinary person does read between the lines

The fact that you did not mean to defame someone is of no consequence. People suing you for damages do not have to prove you have defamed them. You have to prove you have not (unless you can pay them enough money to go away and promise never to do it again).

You cannot defame a dead person, but if what you say hurts their living relatives, they may be able to sue you.

You need to be careful when expressing your point of view. You need to be fair, accurate and balanced. You may make "fair comment" but it must be clear you are giving an 'honestly held' opinion and not stating opinion as a fact.

Helpful phrases can include: "I think", "It seems to me", "In my opinion", "It looks to me as if..." can help – but not always.

If a lawyer's letter arrives on your desk there is no legal defence in saying things such as:

- I made a mistake (don't we all)
- I read it in a magazine (you and the magazine both risk being sued)
- Someone else told me it was true (that's called hearsay and it carries no weight at all – you just risk dragging someone else into the frame)
- I said it was just a rumour (that won't wash either)

If you get the facts wrong, you have no defence in law. You don't have to name someone to defame them. You can also defame a company if it can prove your comment is likely to cause it financial loss. You can also commit defamation if you criticise a group of people (they could all sue you). Discuss the issue or the action, never the person.

What may be protected by freedom of speech in one country may result in a prison sentence (or worse) in another. Laws will be different from one country to another and from one State to another.

Even if you link to a defamatory statement from your website to someone else's you may be liable for damages (and that includes social media links too).

So while this chapter may put you in the right direction, you need to know what you can and can't say in your country and play it safe should you want to start criticising people (alive or dead) and companies / corporation in general.

If you really want to get up to speed with media law then there are plenty of online courses run by organisations such as the Poynter Institute and the Centre for Media Freedom may also be a source of help.

It's not all bad news though. There are defences that can generally be used if challenged. These include: honest opinion; that you are factually correct; and while there is a limitation period for people to raise an action against you, it may not apply if a judge allows the 'out of time' action to proceed (because there is no way the offended party could have heard your podcast in the normal course of their day).

You might want to consider taking out insurance so you can be represented should someone take an action against you, placing your valuables in a family trust to protect them, and seek professional legal advice from a media lawyer who can explain the basics. Also be aware of broadcast standards / regulations in your country.

Financial advice and investments

You need to be really careful when talking about money and investments. There are a bundle of official organisations who will come down on you like a tonne of bricks if you tell people that buying anything is a good investment, safe haven, or a way to make money.

It is common that people have to be registered financial advisors to offer advice on investments, insurance and financial products.

Consumer protection

If you discuss any products or services you must be able to back up any claims you make with factual evidence if challenged. Giving your opinion is one thing. Stating something as absolute fact is another.

However, a lot can come down to the perception of the listener, and if they feel your opinion is presented as fact, and it isn't, then you risk facing trouble via advertising standards or some such consumer group.

Stick to facts and phrases such as "according to the manufacturer..." and quote its claims correctly.

For further information on media law, see:
- https://goo.gl/89rKeS and https://goo.gl/9dJaqg

Podcast Libraries

Podcast libraries include Apple, TuneIn, Spreaker, Stitcher, iHeartRadio and anywhere else you can find truckloads of podcasts.

The key thing to remember is that few of these podcast libraries store your MP3 files on their servers, they merely link to the files where they *are* stored, via your RSS podcast feed, and draw upon them when someone clicks 'play' or download on a website somewhere.

You won't know what your podcast RSS feed is until you have your website organised or have your files hosted with a firm such as Libsyn, Blubrry or some other podcast hosting service.

So it's one step at a time. Make your podcast, upload it, and then get the RSS feed. FYI – one podcast RSS feed will link to all your podcasts (you don't need an RSS feed for each podcast episode).

Here are some of the places to send your podcast RSS feed to:

Apple: http://bit.ly/1hrjvHs
Stitcher: stitcher.com/content-providers
GooglePlay: https://play.google.com/music/podcasts/publish
TuneIn: www.tunein.com/broad-casters
Spreaker: www.spreaker.com (offers access to iHeartRadio and YouTube)
Doubletwist: www.doubletwist.com/contact

Almost everything else: www.podcast411.com/page2.html

Hosting providers

Blubrry: www.blubrry.com
PodOMatic: www.podomatic.com
Libsyn: www.libsyn.com *(Liberated Syndication, in case you were wondering)*

What I have found is that once a podcast is listed with the main players it is picked up by all manner of other distributors too.

Key take away
Send your podcast RSS feed to as many podcast libraries as you can.

Your copyright

Anything you create is copyrighted by default. There is no form to fill out to establish ownership. However, I recommend you adopt one of the Creative Commons licenses that sets out how your podcast can be used (www.CreativeCommons.org) by people who may download it.

The CC license I use is Attribution-NonCommercial-NoDerivatives 4.0 International and there is a note – for listeners – on my website explaining how they can use my podcasts if they download them.

Copyright is very simple to understand. If you create something that is your own original work (unique to you), then you own the copyright to it.

Therefore, it is likely (unless you are reading out someone else's text, or are employed to podcast by someone else), that you will own the rights to your work (the words spoken and the audio recording).

Having said that, if you are employed, even as a freelancer or contractor, check your employment contract to see who owns the things you create – is it the employer or you, or something in between?

Distributing podcasts under a CC license helps people understand that the work is owned by the creator, and puts restrictions on how podcasts may be used by people who download them.

For example, you may not want your podcast to have commercials added to it by someone else and then re-posted somewhere else or broadcast without your permission. You may not want sections cut out, or to have sections of your podcast form a part of someone else's podcast or radio show.

Of course physically preventing someone from using your work without permission is impossible, but if you discover your work is being used without permission then you can at least let them know they have breached your copyright because those rights have been asserted.

Consider adding a copyright notice in each podcast; "This podcast is copyright [your name] and can't be re-used without prior written permission".

See www.CreativeCommons.org to decide which one (if any) of its free licenses is best for you to adopt.

You need to take your copyright seriously (no one else will). Think of the worst case scenario such as it being copied and placed on someone else's website with adverts cut into it promoting a firm you would never want to endorse or support.

Or to find them behind a paywall with someone else charging to access your podcasts. Honestly, I have seen it happen and in this digital world it can be hard if not impossible to be compensated for a breach of this kind.

You can't hope to stop scum bags stealing your work if that's what they set out to do, but your starting point is to establish your ownership so everyone knows the conditions of accessing your work.

There are idiots out there too. I once had a PDF book for sale and discovered one purchaser was sending it around to all their mates. I asked her what she thought she was doing (breaching my copyright)?

"Oh I am just helping you get the book out there, I thought you would be grateful." She appeared to have no concept that every time she gave *my* book away it was a potential lost sale for me. They walk among us.

Their copyright

Let's assume for a moment you have a podcast that reviews new music. As soon as you feature someone else's work in your podcast you risk breaching the owner's copyright (that's why radio stations pay royalty fees to music companies and artists).

But if you are going to critique their work, the Fair Use/Fair Dealing laws apply. But how much of their music can you feature before you risk being accused of breaching copyright?

As far as I know there is no one-size fits all rule or legal definition of what Fair Use is when it comes to relying on it as a defence for a claim of copyright infringement. So tread carefully. Be reasonable.

See: http://fairuse.stanford.edu/overview/fair-use/four-factors/

Key take away
When you create something original you own the rights to it.

Royalty free music

The term 'royalty free music' can be confusing for people who read 'free music' as opposed to what it actually means – 'royalty free' music.

So what does the term 'royalty free' mean? In short it means that once you own a license to use a piece of music you should not need to pay anyone any royalties every time *you* use it.

With royalty free music there is often a high up-front cost for the track, but nothing more to pay – no matter how many times you (as a license holder) uses it.

Normally, royalty free music is sold under a license; i.e, as an owner of the license, you are free to use the music for podcasts, radio, TV, film soundtracks etc, but you can't sell or give away the track because you don't own it. You only have a license to use it.

There are plenty of people around who will provide music to you without charge, or any ongoing costs.

Some release their music under a Creative Commons license – there are various versions of this license – so always check the fine print to avoid an angry email alleging breach of copyright/license.

Some music creators also give their work away free, but on condition it is listed as being used with copyright agencies, so the creator gets money from them every time it is used.

It can all get very confusing I know, but if you buy a track from a reputable supplier then all should be fine. If in doubt' tell them how you plan to use the music and confirm no more fees are payable once you get it.

And if you are handy with music software (lot's of PCs and Macs come with music creation apps) you can create your own little ditty and have something completely original (give it a go!).

Software

Scratch the surface of the podcasting community and you'll likely read that people boast about using top end software such as Adobe Audition and SoundForge.

Truth is that people who claim to use high-priced apps likely were already using them for other purposes and didn't spend up large just to do a podcast.

Because podcasting doesn't require apps with advanced features. You just want to record your voice and maybe (it is not compulsory) add a bit of music for taste.

That said, here are a few pointers to get you going and my recommendation for starters is the free-for-any-platform multi-track audio recording/editing app Audacity.

Free music

www.betterwithmusic.com

www.freemusicarchive.org

Paid-for music

www.newsbeds.com

www.gettyimages.co.nz/music

www.audiojungle.net

Audio editing software

www.audacity.sourceforge.net

www.nch.com.au/wavepad

www.mediahuman.com

www.hindenburg.com

www.reaper.fm

GarageBand, free with your Mac

Worth looking at

www.commedia.org.uk

www.internet-radio.com

www.rogueamoeba.com/freebies

Key take away
You likely already have the software you need on your PC.

Ending your podcast

It might seem strange writing about ending a podcast in a book all about starting one. But rest assured, each podcast has a set life.

You can tell when your enthusiasm starts to wain when you skip a week and don't give it a second thought and feel really great that you got those hours back to do something more enjoyable. When it is all becoming a chore, and the rot has set in, it's time to give it the chop.

Plenty of podcasters just leave the last episode hanging and subscribers wait to see if a new episode will arrive (just because they don't contact you doesn't mean they are not waiting).

It's kind of OK to leave it fluid if you are hedging your bets as it gives you the option to start again after a period away.

But it's also good to let listeners know that you are taking time out and give them a date for when you will be back, or that this is the last episode – for now.

So if you really have done your dash, make a final episode to let your listeners know and say cheerio, and thanks for all the fish.

Having ended a podcast my advice is to leave everything in place. Don't delete the podcasts or cancel accounts / RSS feeds because next week, or next month, you may want to start podcasting about something else. In which case all you need do is update the artwork and show description and start again. Or if you are really keen, set up a second podcast RSS feed and have two out there.

Making the podcasts will not have been a waste of time. You'll be able to look back at all the lessons learned and the next podcast (there is always a next one) will be even easier to get going.

Key take away
There's always another beginning. Never stop starting.

WordPress websites

First off, you do not need a website to share your podcasts. You can use any one of dozens of podcast hosting firms who will give you a unique RSS feed for you to share with any podcast library / sharing service you care to name. There are plenty of podcasters who do not have a dedicated podcast website or any website at all (shame really).

But I'm guessing you may need a website if you haven't already got one, in which case, please allow me to recommend a WordPress.org website.

Years ago I inherited an old style hard coded (HTML) site and frankly it was a pig to work with. I figured there must be a better way than paying someone $50 to change a headline and so started Googling. I came across a few CMS options; WordPress, Drupal and Joomla. I tried them all but clicked with WordPress in a trice.

WordPress is a free CMS (content management system) that provides an easy-to-use website admin area (the place one logs into to create new posts and make customised changes to the look and feel of a website).

The standard WordPress instal comes with a basic theme (look and feel of what visitors see) and most of the functionality you will need. But you will want more (it's human nature – we always want more).

There are hundreds of fully working free themes from the WordPress library to download as well as hundreds of plugins that add things such as contact forms, audio players, photo slideshows...you name it. I have built dozens of WordPress sites and wouldn't use anything else.

Many website hosting firms provide an easy way to install WordPress as part of the plans they offer. So research web hosting firms, ask about their support for WordPress and dive in.

The Blubrry plugin is made for podcasters and comes with a link to have your podcast appear on Apple's podcasting app (you will need to have an account and have your artwork ready before you submit it).

Final thoughts

We are in the advanced stages of a digital revolution that has knocked newspaper and magazine publishing for six, forced TV stations to start streaming content via the internet and now radio stations are sending their broadcasts over the internet too. Cable TV anyone?

Add to the mix tablets, computers, internet radio receivers, the smartphone and the growing internet connectivity of cars, 5G, and we can see where all this is taking us.

Podcasters have a world of opportunity before them and a global audience hungry for fresh, original and high quality content. All you have to do is provide it to them. Every week.

Play on demand has been adopted by mainstream broadcasters who have had their hands forced by people who want to listen to what they want, when they want, and on the device they want – a thirst for choice that's quenched by faster, cheaper, broadband and free wifi services.

It is an exciting time for creators such as you. A golden time, not unlike the birth of popular radio itself when DJs took to the air playing their (not marketing's) choice of music in the 1950/60s.

Podcasting can be great fun, give you an easy way to share your passion and expertise, and provide a great way to connect with people around the world. Perhaps even an income!

The online audio revolution is well underway and whether you are podcasting to entertain people, comment on the week's news or share industry information, there are billions of people waiting for you. They just don't know it yet.

You owe it to yourself to make the best podcasts you can, offer interesting content, quality recordings, and polished to the highest standard you can achieve.

Do this at regular intervals, remain consistent and reliable, don't offer more than you can deliver and stick to your knitting. You can do it, and the only thing stopping you is you. You do not need anyone's permission to be a success.

Listener feedback

Try not to take any feedback too seriously. Some of it will make your head swell with pride (take this kind of feedback with a pinch of salt).

Other feedback may be venomous and hateful, don't take it to heart as it will distract you from where you need to be. Nasty feedback often comes from unhappy people who want to spread their misery around (ignore them).

Feedback is good (people are listening). It is worth reading it all because someone may have a valid point or an idea that can help you.

However, good or bad, I often reply with a standard "thanks for your feedback" email. And it is always interesting to see which emails bounce back because some coward has used a fictitious address in my website's contact form.

The future

Podcasters have a world of opportunity, so long as we have a free and open internet. And that is something some telcos and governments are trying to stop. We must all play our part in keeping a single tier internet service in place and prevent other people from picking and choosing what we can see, hear and read online. Consumers should be the judge, not corporations or governments.

Media freedom *is* under threat from governments and corporations, they'd like nothing more than to control the narrative and manage / filter what people see and hear. Nanny knows best.

Unfortunately, it is only when those freedoms are lost that people will realise what's happened – and clawing it back is always a challenge that relies on political will to have it restored.

Creators such as us need to remain vigilant and strongly challenge those who aim to restrict our rights to freedom of expression. Freedom is too easily given away for a promise of greater protection. Protect the net.

Many thanks, I hope this book helps you, and good luck,

Steve Hart

Worth reading

Media freedom
www.cpbf.org.uk/
www.newsmediauk.org/Current-Topics/Press-Freedom
www.freedomhouse.org/issues/internet-freedom

Edison Research USA
Short: https://bit.ly/2JNtKNB
Original: www.edisonresearch.com/the-podcast-consumer-2019/

Edison Research Australia
Short: https://goo.gl/WHfuQN
Original: www.edisonresearch.com/podcast-consumer-australia-2017/

File downloads statistics
Short code: https://goo.gl/ZLCGiH
Original: https://iabtechlab.com/specifications-guidelines/podcast-measurement-guidelines/

Interactive Advertising Bureau
https://www.iab.com/

Fair use
fairuse.stanford.edu/overview/fair-use/four-factors/

International Podcasting Day
internationalpodcastday.com/

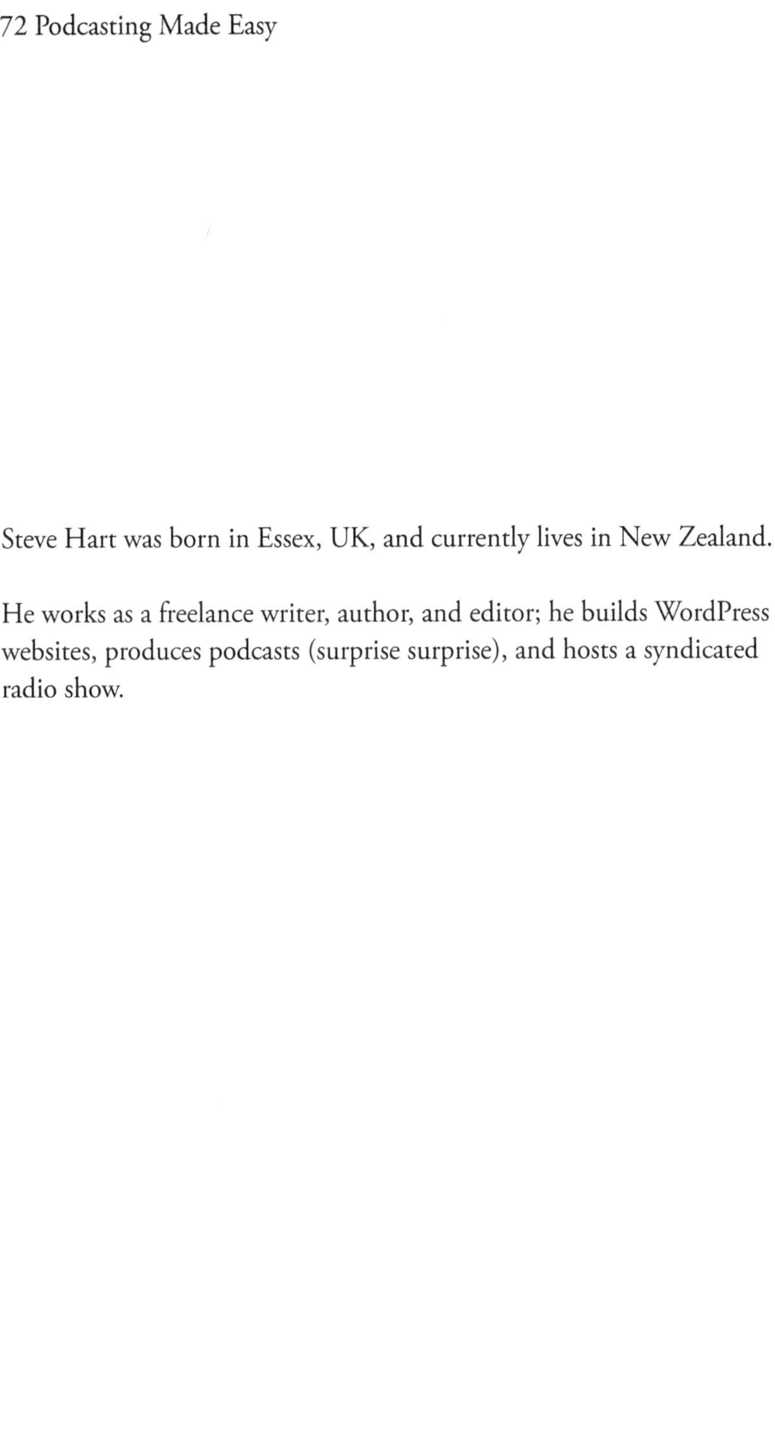

Steve Hart was born in Essex, UK, and currently lives in New Zealand.

He works as a freelance writer, author, and editor; he builds WordPress websites, produces podcasts (surprise surprise), and hosts a syndicated radio show.